MW01479712

ℐnspiration

—•═•—

May your day
be inspired.

Ruth

To Sharon... Xmas 2016

damajune

Inspiration

To Open Your Heart, Awaken Your Mind,
and Touch Your Soul

by

Ruth Marcus, PhD

Wide ● Awake
PUBLISHING

INSPIRATION
To Open Your Heart, Awaken Your Mind, and Touch Your Soul
by Ruth Marcus, PhD

Published by Wide Awake Publishing
P.O. Box 2650, Sequim, WA 98382-2650 USA
www.WideAwakePublishing.com

Edited by Diana Sommerville, Port Angeles, WA

ISBN: 978-0-9766004-0-4

TABLE OF CONTENTS

—•••—

Dedicated to my loving
family, friends, colleagues,
daily inspiration email recipients,
and
my special golden retriever pals,
Rumi & Porter,
who have inspired me with
lessons on
unconditional love.

———◆———

I wish to acknowledge, with deep appreciation,
the generosity of the following people.
Each has given me support and encouragement
in meaningful ways, and for that
I am deeply grateful.

THANK YOU...

Barbara W., Barbara L., Carolina, Chuck,
Craig, Denise & Gerry,
Diana, Ed & Mary, Holly,
Jeanine Lucille, Mark & Bob,
Mary D., Maureen,
Michelle H., Mike & BJ,
Ross, Rev. Susanne, Ted & Arlette,
Tony & Mike, Sherry, Trudy A.

Ruth Marcus (known as Dr. Ruth in the "circuit of inspiration") was raised in a small, Swiss community in southern Wisconsin. With an insatiable curiosity to explore life, she headed west with only a backpack on her back. San Francisco (and mostly Marin County) would become her home for the next 30 years. Recently she has been living in the Pacific Northwest, where the beauty, tranquility, and lifestyle allow her to remain highly creative and spiritually nurtured.

Her life continues to inspire many people as she expresses herself as an entrepreneur, teacher, counselor, spiritual guide, artist, and author. She has shown her gifts and talents through graphic design, photography, clothing design and manufacturing, teaching at the Academy of Art in San Francisco, founding five successful businesses, and publishing inspirational and self-help books.

With a Masters Degree in Clinical Psychology and a Doctorate Degree in Religious Studies, Ruth is committed to offering her listening and inquiry skills as a compassionate counselor and teacher. Her work includes facilitating and teaching such topics as wisdom training, communication and relationship building, and spiritual inquiry.

Ruth has volunteered and supported people who face life-threatening illnesses and those who grieve from loss. This volunteer work has been with the International Center for Attitudinal Healing in Sausalito, CA and Hospice of Clallam County, WA.

Deeply spiritual, Ruth integrates various philosophies and practices and believes that one's spiritual life is truly a path of learning how to live peacefully. "I cannot say that there is only *one* way. There are many paths that lead to inner peace. Whether you believe in God or Allah or Buddha or Quan Yin or a Higher Power or Nature, it is your spiritual life — your spiritual path.

"I have learned so many truths through the observation of nature," says Ruth. "In my willingness to become quiet and contemplative, I learn to see things from many perspectives, gaining insight and feeling deeply connected to all things. There is a lovely and mysterious energy that surrounds every thing in life, and I prefer to honor this sacredness without assigning it to any one religion."

INTRODUCTION

from the author

This book began in 2001 as a free, daily inspiration service on the internet. I decided that I wanted to follow Eleanor Roosevelt's example to live and believe that one person's life can make a difference.

In considering the immediacy and power of the internet, and its capacity to reach many people in a split second, I decided to commit to writing original, inspirational "one-liners." My plan was to send them to friends, colleagues, and family members every morning, Monday through Friday.

What I didn't anticipate was the growth of the email list. Recipients found value in the daily inspiration and began sharing it with their friends and family members. Over the course of four years, I have continued to write every morning, and the email list continues to grow.

I am thrilled when people respond with
gratitude, humor, and thoughtful comments.

One Memorial day, I wrote and sent the
following:

A Day of Remembrance.

Let all soldiers of war, who live and who have died,
  stand shoulder to shoulder and circle the earth.
Let all victims of war, who live and who have died,
  stand shoulder to shoulder and circle the earth.
Let all those who have loved these people, who live
  and who have died, stand shoulder to shoulder
  and circle the earth.
Let all of us, together, stand shoulder to shoulder
  and circle the earth remembering the beauty of
  who we are as our tears cleanse all souls from
  the past, from the present, from the future.

A recipient responded: "This is great! Very
moving. This should be carved in black marble
on the war memorial in Washington DC…Ms.
Lin, the young (Chinese-American) designer of
the Vietnam War Memorial would love this."

I am fascinated with the personal relationships that I have established through these
writings. If I miss sending out inspiration for a
day, there are people who email and ask,
"Where are you? Are you okay?" And nearly
every day, at least one person writes asking,
"How did you know what I needed to hear this
morning?"

One day, a woman wrote, "What state are
you writing from?"

"I'm in the great state of Washington,
and where are you?"

The woman replied, "I'm a senator from
the great state of Georgia, and thank you for
your daily words of encouragement."

To my amazement, my inspirations had
reached that level of our government —
certainly a place where a bit of inspiration
might be of great benefit!

Another inquiry arrived from a faculty member from Wesleyan University asking permission to include some of the inspirational writings in a workshop, and I often receive requests to include my quotes in newsletters. "I love quoting Dr. Ruth," said a minister. "I hope you are putting them in a book."

After my first year, another recipient wrote, "You have just completed your first book."

I asked, "What do you mean?"

The response "You have just written one year's worth of daily inspiration — that's a book!"

Clearly, when I started writing the daily inspirations and emailing them every morning, I had no idea how meaningful it would become to so many people.

Four years later, the book you are holding is a compilation of "the best" of over a thousand writings — all sent out in the early morning hours. I now know that one person's life *does* make a difference, and there is a multitude of ways for that to happen.

The lesson I have learned is to simply share your talents, share your strengths, share your wisdom. One kind word, one kind action can make a huge difference in a world that is in great need of kindness.

Love life. Live gratefully,

Ruth

365
Inspirations

1

There is no greater gift
to give a friend
than the truth.

 2

"May I help you?" the cow
asked the sparrow.
And the sparrow rested upon the cow's back.
Lesson: You just never know when
an act of kindness affords
someone a moment's rest.

3

Be yourself.
That's enough.

4

One hundred and eight blades of grass;
multiply them, and they become a
forest of green that tickles your toes.
One hundred and eight acts of kindness;
multiply them, and they become a
forest of gratitude that tickles your soul.

5

When a song fails to rise up,
just hum.

 6

Sitting with owls may be
a wise practice.
Learning to hoot softly
is wisdom.

7

"Shall we dance?" the moon asked the stars,
and each one said yes to the other.
How is it that we humans forget
the simplicity of saying yes, so that
each of us has the opportunity
to join in the dance?

8

I often thought,
and then I noticed my thoughts,
and I became the Thinker.

9

There are many lessons to be gained
in not getting what you want.
Patience is one.

 10

When the soul has an itch,
scratching the surface
will not satisfy the calling.

11

There is a useful tool
for enjoying life:
See it through the eyes of wonder.

12

Giving up
is knowing when to let go.
Giving in
is knowing when to cooperate.

13

Learning to love what you have
is mastery.

 14

When was the last time
you said "I Love You" and then
took the time to listen as each word
reverberated back to your heart?

15

Freedom arises the moment
you recognize that you are bound
by outdated beliefs.

16

Brilliance?
Your willingness to shine
even when you feel tarnished.

17

Transcending the "blues"
is as simple as being willing
to sing the song.

 18

The value of history
is only as good as what you
make of it today.

19

Listening to an ache in your body
is a reminder that listening **prior**
to the ache is a wise lesson to learn.

20

Trust?
Being willing to slide down
a moonbeam and
never concern yourself with falling.

21

Give the best you have
and you will experience
the best of your life.

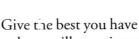

 22

Sing a song of love.
Dissonance becomes harmony.

23

Sound advice:
Don't give any.

24

There is a lovely weaving on display today.
Take a look around
and see how interwoven your life is
with others.

25

Add a handful of gratitude
to a pitcher filled with love.
Blend thoroughly, and life has just become
a very sweet experience.

26

Untruth:
You can't make a difference
in improving life on Earth.
Truth:
You are the difference.

27

Imagine dancing on tree tops!
Now imagine how much you miss out on
simply because you fail to imagine.

28

Need transformed
is a good deed given.

29

With all uncertainty,
learning to sit with it
is the most challenging.

 30

The fork in the road affords you
a choice for new opportunity.
Interesting how many people
remain stuck in the fork.

31

How do you spell relief?
Be who you are.

32

Knowing that all people want to love
and be loved can be your guide
to answering the question,
"What can I do?"

33

That which irritates you
is intended to soften you.

 34

Some things go without saying —
and what a missed opportunity
that frequently is.

35

Celebrating life
each and every day means
your birthday will never be forgotten.

36

Learning to love unconditionally
is the endless process of learning
how to let go.

37

Let go of "whoa"
and you become WOW!

 38

How does one end all the
negative self-talk?
Speak kindly to yourself.

39

Pausing is the best remedy
for speaking unkind words.

40

Turning away from that which you abhor
does not change it.
Facing that which you abhor and seeing it
through the eyes of love
changes everything.

41

Sit with what is
and you will learn more
about the nature of change
than by attempting to change what is.

 42

Searching for love, happiness,
inner peace?
It's time to make a "you" turn.

43

The wonderful thing about
finding the answer
is that, just when you think you've got it,
"it" falls apart, reshapes, reconfigures,
expands, contracts, disintegrates, and
once again the question arises.

44

The nature of vulnerability?
Being willing to expose the shadow
beyond the doubt

45

Living with "if only" keeps
life out of reach.
Living with "yes" means there is
nowhere to reach.

46

Sit next to a river.
It will teach you how to navigate
the endless turns in life.

47

Forgetting is an opportunity
to remember that there is nothing
that needs to be remembered.

48

A simple lesson on how-to-live
from a friendly bumble bee:
"It's a simple matter of Bee-ing."

49

If you can't find a solution
to your problem,
stand on your head.
Sometimes the solution is found
simply by "turning it over."

50

Beauty can be found in what appears
to be the "compost of life."
It is simply a matter of seeing everything
as potential for growth.

Between every conflict there is a space.
It is the space where you decide
whether you are right or wrong.
It is also sacred space where you can decide
to choose peace, and that is the space
where the need to be right or wrong
turns into love.

If you need help in making changes,
let me introduce you to
Will-ingness.

53

Turn your self-talk into self-love,
and you are ready to
walk your talk.

54

Giving and receiving is interesting
to contemplate.
The greatest gift frequently ends up
in the packaging you most
want to avoid.

55

The top of your head is touching the sky.
Is that not enough
to free you from believing
that you have to
reach
for more?

56

Remembering to say "I Love You"
is remembering that it takes very few words
to change the direction you are
going in life.

57

When you encounter a power struggle,
let go of power and
the struggle dissolves immediately.

58

Seeking love?
Listen from within
and that which is sought
will whisper over and over,
"I Love You, I Love You, I Love You."

59

Life is intricately woven.
What would it mean if you
gave up tugging at the threads?

60

Clarity of intention
will readily guide you in the direction
of the results you seek.

61

Expressing gratitude is simple:
Thank you!

 62

Worry is the velcro in life:
an untrained mind
stuck to living only in the future.

63

Beginning again is a wise thing to do.
Begin again, and again, and again.

64

When I was a child,
I questioned everything.
When I became an adult,
I questioned the questions.
Enlightenment is eliminating
the punctuation.

65

There is something about those
prim and proper primroses.
They seem to defy the concept
of frowning.

 66

Attitudinal adjustment?
Sing, hum, or whistle.

67

Walk before me, and I learn how to follow.
Walk behind me, and I learn how to lead.
Walk beside me, and I learn how to
be your friend.

68

Grin and bear it causes
constipation of the soul.
Grin and express it relieves everyone.

69

Being in love is exactly that...
an exquisite state of Being.

70

Being right
is the antithesis of peace.

71

Are you waiting for enlightenment?
The light doesn't turn on my friend,
unless you plug n.

72

One step, two steps,
three steps, more.
Willingness is the key
for opening the door!

73

The quality of this day
depends on how much
you appreciate it.

 74

When you think you have
found the answer to life,
ask another question.

_75_

Look at the world with "soft eyes,"
and all judging, blaming, and resenting
become loving.

_76_

How can you radically improve your life?
Ask yourself,
"Am I living with ease and grace?"

77

Mind-chatter fills space
that is meant to be open space.
No wonder life becomes chaotic —
there is no open space.

 78

Instruction on Practicing Appreciation:
Twinkle, twinkle little star,
I so appreciate who you are.

Catch a falling star?
It just might turn out to be a friend
who bumped into the moon while
attempting to fly.
Life is, after all, trial and error.
Brushing off a little stardust
is a friendly thing to do.

It is in your nature to be happy.
If you're not happy,
it's time to get back to nature.

81

I start to think I'm a buddha-ful person.
Then I remember the tree
and go sit under it and consider what it
means to be Buddha-ful.

82

Censorship:
The error that prevents two hearts
from experiencing intimacy.

83

The saying is,
don't cross the bridge until you come to it.
I still haven't come to the bridge.
Do you think it's time that I start
building my own?

84

To walk your talk is an evolved concept.
It requires that you learn how
to keep your mouth shut
while you maintain balance
between standing still and moving along.

85

When you can look at everyone
without wanting anyone to change,
you have come to appreciate
all of who you are.

 86

Incidentally, it is the little incidents
and what you make of them
that create war.
Is that a co-incidence?

Trusting the outcome means
accepting the present moment as the only
possibility you have for effecting anything.

A miser-soul keeps the heart closed.
A wiser-soul keeps the heart open.
Where the two meet is in the valley of
unconditional love.

89

There is no time like now
to reconcile fear and love.
One is an error in thinking.
The other is what corrects the error.

 90

People whispered,
"She is full of herself."
What are you full of?

91

Learning to stretch involves
more than muscle.
Just how flexible are you?

92

It's no wonder life gets boring.
When was the last time you spent time
just wondering?

93

Frog a-creakin'; fish a-soakin';
    turtle a-pokin'.

Here's a token:
Singing, swimming, crawling —
    three possibilities
of how to go through life.

 94

Instructions for creating joy:
    1. Tickle yourself.
    2. Laugh, laugh, laugh.
    3. Notice how contagious joy is.

95

Smiling is the quickest way
to turn life in an upward direction.

96

Stop focusing on what you don't have
or what you don't like
and you will find yourself happily
focusing on what you have.

97

There is one powerful way to
see yourself through trying times:
stop trying.

 98

Little did any of us know,
when we came to Earth,
that remembering who we are
would be more challenging
than forgetting who we are.

99

The daily news, uncensored,
would be you asking yourself,
"What's up?"

100

Nothing like today
to find out what you didn't do yesterday
and what you are going to put off
for yet another day.
And what exactly is happening today?

101

The sun shines. The moon shines.
And what is getting in the way
of you shining?

 102

There are simple ways
to learn simple things.
Stand up.
Sit down.
Appreciate change.

103

Tip-toeing through the tulips
teaches you how to walk mindfully
through life.

104

This day can be the most meaningful
simply because you decide
to find meaning in it.

105

If you don't want to
give someone the shirt off your back,
try walking in their shoes for a day.

 106

If you are wondering why there are
so many detours in your life,
maybe it is time to notice whose map
you are allowing yourself
to be guided by.

107

Imagination is the engine that
drives every act of creation.
To keep it running smoothly,
you must use it.

108

Pause before you speak,
and you will find you are becoming
a more thoughtful person.

109

Everytime you want to live in fear
because a black cat crossed your path,
ask yourself, "What difference does it
make whether the cat is
black or brown or yellow?"

110

A lesson from frogs:
Croaking in unison makes
a dark night beautifully tolerable.

111

If you weren't so hard on others,
do you think you would be
easier on yourself?
If you weren't so hard on yourself,
do you think you would be
easier on others?

112

The nature of nurture?
A peaceful mind and a loving heart.

117

To become a true peacekeeper,
you must make peace with yourself.

 118

The Zen of mowing the lawn?
One blade of grass at a time.

<u>119</u>

Walking a labyrinth teaches you
that losing your way in life
is virtually impossible.
Put one foot in front of the other
and keep walking.

<u>120</u>

And are you willing
to be willing?

121

A course on death and dying
is mandatory.
You will learn how to
live with uncertainty
and appreciate living.

 122

Skydiving is a lesson in trust and faith.
It teaches you that you have to trust
that your parachute will open,
and that faith comes from being
willing to take the leap.

123

Rub your cheek against the cheek
of someone you love.
Joy-filled physics in action!

124

Awakening with gratitude in your heart
completes the circle of having
gone to sleep with a grateful heart.

125

If you think it's too good to be true,
you obviously aren't willing
to raise the bar and accept
how good it really can be!

 126

If the dance of life is saying,
"Circle to your left,"
why do you resist the instructions?

127

If you find that it is difficult for you
to receive,
take a look at the conditions
you may be attaching to your giving.

128

Change requires one
essential ingredient:
making the decision.

129

Getting along with people is simple.
Let go of your expectations.

 130

Dirty laundry affords many lessons:
The nature of sorting and agitating,
and finally the joy of tumbling
in the warm cycle.

131

Some people seek fortune.
Others recognize how fortunate they are
just being alive.

132

Silence:
The practice of keeping ones mouth closed
while simultaneously quieting one's mind.

133

There are times when just sitting
is enough.
And, learning to just sit with what is
is a practice in patience.

134

Worrying is the withering
of one's willingness
to let go.

135

If dandelions were really
daffodils in disguise, do you suppose
we would stop seeing them as weeds?
How can we apply this in our
human relations?

136

Counting your blessings
requires one thing:
Leave the counting house.
Blessings are everywhere!

137

When looking through the window,
remember there is a more
expansive view of life —
get out in it.

 138

There is one simple way of
creating a circle of peace —
join hands.

139

Waiting for everything to be just right
will leave you waiting
for the rest of your life.

140

Love grows exponentially,
based on your willingness to
give and receive it.

141

When it comes to being responsible,
ask yourself,
"Am I willing and able to respond?"

 142

When a door of opportunity opens,
remember that it
didn't do it on its own.

143

Me thinks that attachment is about
wringing your insides out.
Let go and see how soft your
belly, heart, and mind become.

144

I have never met a tree
that hasn't welcomed me to sit and
carry on a conversation.
If only we humans were so available
to each other

145

Today is the day to prioritize.
What have you placed before love?

 146

If something stinks,
it is a good idea to see whose business
you have put your nose into.

147

To see a twinkle in someone's eyes
is a reminder that it is
a reflection of the light that
shines within you.

148

All good things end.
Then all good things begin.
Let it be. Let it be. Let it be.

149

Human greatness is like a mountain.
It does not place value
on its position in life.

 150

When you fear going forward,
know that going backward
only makes going forward
a greater distance the next time.

151

Choose to laugh
and your belly will remind you
that happiness is a
full-body experience.

152

Living today with a smile on your face
is optional.
So is frowning.
What's your choice?

153

Personal integrity requires
that you make sure the shoes
you are walking in actually are yours.

 154

When nothing seems to be working
in your life,
trust that even that
is an important part of your life.

155

When you think you have
nothing appropriate to wear,
try a smile.

156

A swallow stopped by this morning
and asked if she could build a nest in
the eaves of my roof.
In a flash, I realized how much work
I still have to do to be
a genuinely hospitable person.

157

If you complain about the
grass growing too fast,
maybe it's time to look within
and see what's holding up *your* growth.

158

"Get a life" means taking responsibility
for living your life
rather than trying to live
everyone else's.

159

Lesson from a guru cat:
Arch your back.
Meow three times.
Walk away from it.

160

Imagine that you made it all up.
Poof!
Trouble is gone.

161

There are so many small ways
to tell someone that you care.
Start with "I appreciate you."

 162

Just when you think you've seen everything,
you turn another life corner.
Voila! Beauty and love show up
in an even more incredible way.

163

When you doubt yourself,
remember that doubt is faith
turned inside out.
You get to turn it around.

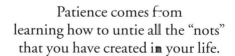

164

Patience comes from
learning how to untie all the "nots"
that you have created in your life.

165

When you wonder if you
love someone unconditionally,
ask yourself,
"Am I willing to let go?"

 166

Your mind is a magnet.
Think a thought
and notice what gets attached to it.

167

The sacred practice of honoring change
is letting go of what was.

168

Sing praises of gratitude
and the whole world
becomes a more peaceful place.

169

One thing about life
is that it teaches us to get on with it.

170

Those who annoy you
are your spiritual teachers.
When there are no more annoying people,
your diploma arrives.

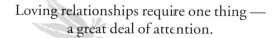

171

Loving relationships require one thing —
a great deal of attention.

172

Self-acceptance begins with
letting go of the idea that
you have to become
better, smarter, richer, wiser.

173

And what wondrous adventure
will you set out upon today?

174

Life is like a toaster —
turn up the heat too high
and you get burned.

175

Star gazing *
You, remembering to keep
the sparkle in your eyes.

176

Putting it off until tomorrow
is one way of
collecting a lot of junk in your life.

177

When your life feels like it is all up hill,
consider turning around.

 178

To awaken with a grateful heart
is assurance that you
recognize this day as a gift.

179

Imitate a frog.
Take the leap!

180

The sun is up!
Now it's your turn to shine.

181

Life challenges may appear insurmountable
but remember that it is only your mind
that has blown them out of proportion.

182

Be gentle. Be kind.
Be generous. Be forgiving.
Now, look in the mirror
and acknowledge
what an incredible Be-ing you are.

183

Getting from where you are
to where you want to be
requires one thing:
intentionality.

184

Listening is not just done with your ears.
When you listen with your heart,
it requires that you
fully engage in being with another person.

185

Let bitterness be transformed
by the fruits of your labor.

 186

Stand under a shower of positive thinking
and every cell of your body
will radiate peace and well-being.

Scientifically, evaporation is the process
of turning liquid into vapor.
On a soul level, it is the process of
changing suffering into grace.

Children call dandelions "pretty flowers."
Then someone tells them they are weeds.
Aren't you grateful that you grew up
to realize you can
choose how to view all things?

189

Oil and water do not mix.
What are you attempting to combine
that does not mix with ease?

190

Impatience with others
demonstrates the degree of patience
that you extend to yourself.

191

A beautiful day is
based on your willingness
to see beauty.

192

Never question the meaning of
taking a few steps backwards.
After all, dancing through life gracefully
requires a full range of motion.

193

What would be different
in your life
if you were impeccably honest?

194

Casting the first stone
is sometimes a grain of sand.
Pay attention to what you consider
an insignificant thought, word or deed!

195

Temptation is an opportunity
to practice discernment.

196

When thunder occurs,
welcome the vibrations overhead.
When the earth shakes,
welcome the vibrations underfoot.
When love is expressed,
welcome the vibrations of
body, mind and soul.

197

A peaceful heart
is one that knows when to speak
and
when to remain silent.

198

When you come upon trouble,
ask yourself,
"Who says this is trouble?"

199

"Why do people continue to
attack one another?"
A voice from deep within responds,
"Stop attacking yourself and
there will be no attacks on anyone else."

200

If you're struggling to solve the riddle,
become the riddle.

201

When lightning dances across the horizon
like some grand and glorious ballerina,
how could you complain of
gray skies?

 202

Let your words
be intended
as loving gifts.

203

There is little time to waste
when it comes to
expressing love.

204

Walk gracefully through the dark
and you will have come
to understand the nature of light.

205

How could you ever doubt there is
a purpose for you in life?
Your purpose is as simple as
love and be loved.

 206

Doubt is what you do
when you have momentarily forgotten
that the answer is within you.

207

There are three very simple ways
to become peaceful —
let go, let go, let go.

208

What makes you think you
have to wait for happiness?
It is wrapped up
in every moment of the day.
It's the gift of life.

209

There are many ways to do many things,
but there is only one way to do your life.
Whole-heartedly.

 210

Even if you have given up
a thousand times before,
begin again.

211

"This too shall pass."
Why are you resisting?

212

Forgiveness is an interesting practice
involving no one but you.

213

Quiet your mind,
and notice how your heart begins to speak
with loving kindness.

 214

Be mindful of your own pace
and you are well on your way to
marching to your own drum.

215

While you sit there wondering
what you can do to change the situation,
the situation is changing.

216

When it comes to the
School of Life,
how many times do you find yourself
repeating certain courses?

217

There s no last hurrah
when you are willing to live your life
with enthusiasm.

 218

There is nothing more important
than grace —
except knowing that it resides within
gratitude.

<u>**219**</u>

A bouquet of flowers may be beautiful
and the heart that brought them
is equally beautiful.

<u>**220**</u>

Moving beyond your perceived limitations
is an act so courageous that
not only do you benefit,
but you inspire others
to follow you.

221

There is no R$_x$ more powerful
than laughter.
Tickle yourself to wellness.

 222

Aging is nothing more than
accepting the deciduous nature of life.

223

An ounce of prevention may work
and other times it may take
a pound of prevention.

224

Before you speak,
before you take action,
ask yourself one question:
"Am I allowing love to be my guide?"

225

If you find yourself with
FedEx friendships
(those that deliver the next day),
ask yourself what needs to change
in order for them to show up today.

 226

Stress is based on
wanting to be somewhere
other than here.

227

Include love in every thought
and you are free of fear.

228

Being mindful of the words you use
will keep you conscious
of the power of choice.

229

Replace "It's too good to be true" with
"It's so good that I know it's true."
Willingness to receive brings great gifts.

230

If your decision was an error,
learning from it
is the next appropriate decision.

231

If you remember to look
through the eyes of wonder,
life will remain forever interesting.

232

Breathing deeply
clears out emotional debris.

233

To be free,
one must examine and integrate
two concepts:
independence and interdependence.

 234

Some things are better left unsaid.
When it comes to gratitude,
it is best said.

235

In counting your friends,
have you included yourself?

236

If you doubt what to do,
consider what *not* to do.

237

Meeting anyone half-way takes initiative.
Ego keeps you from being
the first to take the initiative.

238

To invest your life energy wisely,
ask yourself,
what purpose will this action serve?

239

Telling the truth may create great waves,
but without waves of truth,
the beach becomes littered
with emotional debris.

240

Count the number of times
you say "I should"
and you will find out
how many times you won't.

241

The greatest satisfaction
comes from living simply —
simply by choosing to be incredibly
grateful for your life.

242

Integrity 101:
Say what you mean and do what you say.

243

Celebrating life
is the practice of honoring
each and every breath as the most
exquisite gift you will ever receive.

244

The creation of peace
requires only one thing:
you living it.

245

Smile and you are on an
upward trend toward
experiencing happy.

246

If you are so concerned
about what others think,
you are failing to think for yourself.

247

If you only learn how to
waltz through life,
you will have little appreciation
for fox-trotting.

248

Sink your teeth into life
and you are bound to find out
how tasty life really is.

249

Laughing is the organic action
of shaking yourself free of worry.

 250

Stepping away from something
can be a good choice
as long as you don't fall off a cliff.

251

Sometimes life is a laborious symphony.
Sometimes life is a dazzling aria.
It is your willingness to sit with it
that allows you to appreciate the subtleties.

252

Clap your hands three times.
Now ask yourself,
"To whom do I owe this applause?"

253

A windfall only happens when you
allow yourself to be blown over
by the good grace of life.

 254

If the weight of the world
is on your shoulders,
stand on your head.

255

There is nothing wrong with
asking for help.
How you accept the response
is what matters.

256

You are every bit as beautiful
as every beautiful thing you can imagine.

257

Make today a worry-free day.
See everything as an opportunity
rather than a challenge.

 258

To truly know
Wind, Fire, Earth and Water,
you must be willing to be
blown over, burned, walked upon
and finally go with the flow.

259

If the pot is cracked, consider yourself
blessed with what some people
spend thousands of dollars on:
a drip system.

260

Never doubt the importance
of who you are on this earth.
The oak stands mighty and strong;
the willow bends and weeps.
Neither doubts its importance.

261

Verbal celibacy requires
quieting the voice and the mind.
It is the practice of listening
to your inner truth.

 262

Observation is the precursor
to eliminating your suffering.

263

Being firm
and flexible
are aspects of a loving heart.

264

There is one thing about
hot temperatures —
remove the "temper"
and everything changes.

265

Thinking with your heart
relieves mental frenzy.

 266

An open mind
is the doorway to
clarity of observation.

267

The nature of "humble"
is letting go of the belief
that the show won't go on without you.

268

If your life seems ho-hum,
take out the "ho" and learn to hum.

269

When you feel like a klutz,
introduce yourself to Grace.

 270

Nature provides endless shades of green
so that we might remember one thing —
the spectrum of possibility is endless.

If you think your life isn't important,
tell me who you think you are
without it.

Bunnies are like untamed thoughts —
proliferating until
completely out of control.

273

There is a little-known secret
to living life with ease:
Learn to live with the mystery of it.

274

In a vision of leaping through
fields of poppies and daisies,
I am reminded that
every leap of faith
involves a field of inner beauty.

275

If there is something in your life
that you can't stand,
sit down.
Your perspective will change immediately.

276

"I can't do this" is just another way
of saying, "I am unwilling."

277

Navigating through a life challenge
requires one important quality:
willingness.

278

The morning sun rises.
The evening sun sets.
Life is simple
when you get into the rhythm of it.

279

Longing for clarity in your life?
Be with the fog you are in
and your presence
raises you, naturally, to clarity.

280

If you are thirsty for something in life,
notice where you are.
Then notice that the path you are on
doesn't lead to the fountain.

281

How many times do you
find yourself saying,
"I should do this"?
It is the "should" that is between you
and getting it done.

 282

The concept of too much can only exist
if you believe in too little.
Somewhere in between is enough.

283

Bringing your heart to the table
means that you are willing
to prepare a cornucopia of possibilities
where love serves you and others.

284

Don't worry.
Be happy.
If you can't follow these instructions,
be prepared.

285

The morning songs of bird friends
remind me to awaken
and join them —
singing a song of gratitude.

 286

This is a grand and wonder-filled day.
It is wise person who
decides to enjoy it.

287

You are a field of energetic light.
It is up to you to glow.

288

What time of the day
will you remember
that the only important moment
is now?

289

The simple act of walking a dog
is a spiritual experience.
You get to ask yourself,
"Who is leading whom?"

 290

I met an old woman who lived in a shoe.
She really knew how to
walk the talk.

291

In a nanosecond, you have the ability
and the responsibility
to leap from the mundane
to the extraordinary.
Leap, my dearest, leap!

292

Gratitude expressed
is a ride upon the wings of a dove.

293

Every kind word you speak,
and every good deed you do today,
adds to the quality of life
for all people everywhere.

294

A glimpse of reality
requires that you open your eyes
and see what's in front of you.

295

The cry of a hawk provides
a worthwhile lesson:
When distressed,
remember that soaring is still possible.

296

There is not one thing
you cannot change.
It is your mind that
causes you to believe otherwise.

297

If a loaf of bread contains life,
you, my friend, contain the yeast
to make it rise to a new level.

 298

Lesson from a child:
When you grow tired of life,
do something simple;
lie down with a warm blankie
and take a little nap.

299

The very act of waking up every morning
is affirmation enough that
there is a purpose to it all.
It is our mission to live it!

300

Even when you mumble in silence,
you are creating a disturbance.

301

When your suffering feels like
you just can't endure anymore —
it's time to give up the suffering.

302

Being fully present takes nothing
yet it gives everything.

303

There is nothing you need do
other than love yourself.
If each of us did that,
we would have no enemies.

304

Smiling is the act of
turning everything that was down
to up.

305

Focus on that which is not a problem
and you will have not one problem
in your life.

 306

Inspiration is what comes
bubbling up
when mind-babbling ceases.

Hesitation —
a pause, or a missed opportunity?

Creation?
A cow jumps over the moon.
Is she creating or following the Milky Way?

309

When you feel low on energy,
notice where you are shorting yourself.

310

Life is a bowl of cherries.
And sometimes life gives you lemons
and you make lemonade.
Just remember, baking bread requires
a couple of risings, so don't ever give up!

311

Mumbling under your breath
creates a foul smell in the air.
Speak your truth and sweetness prevails.

312

Appreciating this moment means
being aware of it.

313

If you find yourself side-tracked,
remember
you're the conductor of the train.

314

Hesitation is
tripping at the threshold of trust.

315

Learning to trust?
Open. Pause. Open. Pause.
It is the process of
gently letting go of fear
and opening to love.

316

A garden of kindness
is cultivated through
forgiveness, acceptance,
and appreciation.

317

Do a daily laundering —
wring out the excesses in your life.

 318

I once thought candy was
the sweetest thing in life.
Then I tasted life.

319

Choose your friends well.
They are the ones that choose you.

320

If you stumble and catch yourself
on the way down,
you remembered how important
a single moment truly is.

321

To become a master of
knowing how to toot your horn,
you must first develop
an appreciation for the orchestra.

322

Be-laboring and Be-moaning
are nothing more than Be-ing with
obstacles inserted.
Remove the labor and the moan, and
you experience ease and grace.

323

Deep acknowledgment of another
requires you to set aside the obvious
and look for the rich subtleties of character
that few are willing to notice.

324

Camping under the umbrella
of a mushroom requires you to know
how truly enjoyable
one's imagination can be.

325

When you think life is all uphill,
ask yourself if you have
created a mountain.

326

That person who is driving you nuts,
making you so angry?
Ah, yes, that one:
The greatest teacher you were ever
assigned to in your life!

327

Patience.
A moment by moment practice
of living peacefully.

328

An attitude of gratitude
is the power to heal wounded hearts
and the power to heal wounded nations.

329

The Mirror of Life is everywhere.
May I be willing to see another
and recognize myself.

330

Your mission today,
if you decide to accept it,
is to practice intentional kindness.
Kindness generates kindness.

331

Never argue with a cloudy day.
It will be you that ends up in the fog.

332

A simple recipe for breakfast:
Start the day with a bowl full of love,
sprinkled with Gratitude
and Thoughtfulness.
Now, that's fortified!

333

There is nothing scary about
facing fear as long as you
remember
that fear is love in disguise.

334

Making waves is easy.
Calm water requires an understanding
of what it means to be still.

Outdated belief:
"One step forward, two steps back."
Current belief?
"One step forward, one step forward,
one step forward."

Hitting your thumb with a hammer
is nearly as painful as
driving home your point
when it isn't needed or wanted.

337

Silence means
opening yourself
to the vastness of inner peace.

338

Instruction for the day:
Instead of excuses, express gratitude.

339

Telling an untruth to yourself,
and admitting it,
is reclaiming your integrity.
Next step? Forgive yourself.

340

If you want to see what
your future will hold,
pay attention to your current thinking.

341

The river of life
flows through you every moment.
Purifying the river requires that you
eliminate the pollutants in your mind.

342

I noticed a person
whose habits bothered me.
I wanted to change that person.
Then I realized I was looking
in a mirror.

343

To die every moment
is to remember the importance of
living a meaningful life.

344

If you want to harvest love,
you will need to carry
a bottomless basket.

345

Attachment is a study in the nature
of velcro.
Begin with a base that seeks to cling.
Lean into it mindlessly
and you find yourself stuck.

346

Flying is an art.
Remembering that you have wings
is also an art.

347

What's your hurry?
Life isn't going anywhere
without you.

348

Letting go of a problem
involves the physics of
non-attachment.

349

If butterflies questioned
having a purpose in life,
they would become earth-bound
like man.

350

Is there life after death?
Fallen trees answer that question —
each becomes a microcosm
of new growth.

Chaos is nothing more
than believing you are that which
is whirling about.
In truth, you are the calm at the
center of the whirling.

As a child you loved going out in the rain.
It was a wonder.
Is it still a wonder or something that
you complain about?
I wonder how such a thing can happen.

353

Merrily, merrily, merrily, merrily.
Are you enjoying the dream?

354

Counting your money
has very little to do with
being rich.

Summer snow remains in the mountains
because it is not afraid to
embrace the dark side of life.

Life on Earth is about learning to enjoy
the holographic nature of every moment.

357

Sing praises for this day,
and you will discover there are many
who want to sing with you.

358

Courage is the willingness
to see **all** of who you are
and
still look in the mirror every morning
and say, "I love you."

359

Share yourself.
Share your gifts, your talents, your joy,
your laughter, your beauty, your love.
The world has been waiting
to receive you.

360

People seem to trip over three things:
self-blame, self-doubt, self-hate.
Watch your step!

361

North, South, East, West
are simple reminders that
we can change direction
at any moment.

362

With palms turned up, gently place
one hand under the other.
Feel how sweet it is to receive support
from the one person you need
to love the most.

363

Contemplate the nature of a rock
and you will learn much about
the nature of yielding.

364

Tell anyone that you are grateful to be alive,
and you become an activist for life.
Today is it. Celebrate your life!

365

If you don't get what you want,
trust that you are receiving
something that is far more important.

NOTES, REFLECTIONS & THOUGHTS

NOTES, REFLECTIONS & THOUGHTS

NOTES, REFLECTIONS & THOUGHTS

DRAGONFLY

For those of you who are curious about the symbolism of the dragonfly that appears throughout this book, here are several meanings that have been assigned by various cultures.

The dragonfly is a favorite Japanese symbol for strength.

In the Zuni tradition, the dragonfly embodies supernatural powers.

In China, the dragonfly represents summer and instability.

Navaho culture says the dragonfly is symbolic of pure water.

In other traditions, the dragonfly is symbolic of dreams, renewal, and ancient knowledge. It is believed to bring harmony and good fortune.

To order books,
or to contact the author for
inspirational speaking engagements,
please visit
www.wideawakepublishing.com
or email
info@wideawakepublishing.com

———

If you wish to be added
to Dr. Ruth's daily inspiration email list,
please email
Rmarcus@olypen.com.

Wide ● Awake
PUBLISHING

P.O. Box 2650
Sequim, WA 98382
(360) 681-2205